RACE IN AMERICA

WHITE PRIVILEGE

BY M. T. BLAKEMORE

CONTENT CONSULTANT
Eileen O'Brien
Associate Professor of Sociology
Associate Chair, Department of Social Sciences
Saint Leo University, Virginia Campus

Essential Library

ABDOPUBLISHING.COM

Published by Abdo Publishing, a division of ABDO, PO Box 398166, Minneapolis, Minnesota 55439. Copyright © 2018 by Abdo Consulting Group, Inc. International copyrights reserved in all countries. No part of this book may be reproduced in any form without written permission from the publisher. Essential Library™ is a trademark and logo of Abdo Publishing.

Printed in the United States of America, North Mankato, Minnesota
042017
092017

THIS BOOK CONTAINS RECYCLED MATERIALS

Interior Photos: Andrey Popov/Shutterstock Images, 4–5; Shutterstock Images, 7, 14; iStockphoto, 9, 41, 92–93; Cornelius M. Battey/Library of Congress, 12; ullstein bild/Getty Images, 17; Museum of the City of New York/Byron Collection/Archive Photos/Getty Images, 20–21; Bettmann/Getty Images, 24–25; Everett Historical/Shutterstock Images, 27; North Wind Picture Archives, 29; Angela Major/The Janesville Gazette/AP Images, 33; Mike Ledray/Shutterstock Images, 36–37; Randall Hill/KRT/Newscom, 43; Scott Olson/Getty Images News/Getty Images, 46; AP Images, 48–49, 75; Jason Bahr/MoveOn. org Civic Action/Getty Images Entertainment/Getty Images, 51; Martha Irvine/AP Images, 53; Rogelio V. Solis/AP Images, 55; J. Countess/WireImage/Getty Images, 60–61; Peter Mountain/ Walt Disney Pictures/Everett Collection, 65; Twentieth Century Fox Film Corporation/Everett Collection, 66–67; Matt Sayles/Invision/ AP Images, 69; Robert Abbott Sengstacke/Archive Photos/Getty Images, 72–73; Chris Kleponis/picture-alliance/dpa/AP Images, 81; Miles Chrisinger/Icon SMI/NewscomMiles Chrisinger/Icon Sportswire, 84–85; Ricky Carioti/The Washington Post/Getty Images, 99

Editor: Heidi Hogg
Series Designer: Maggie Villaume

PUBLISHER'S CATALOGING-IN-PUBLICATION DATA

Names: Blakemore, M. T., author.
Title: White privilege / by M. T. Blakemore.
Description: Minneapolis, MN : Abdo Publishing, 2018. | Series: Race in America |
    Includes bibliographical references and index.
Identifiers: LCCN 2016962263 | ISBN 9781532110399 (lib. bdg.) |
    ISBN 9781680788242 (ebook)
Subjects: LCSH: Whites--Race identity--Juvenile literature.
Classification: DDC 305--dc23
LC record available at http://lccn.loc.gov/2016962263

CONTENTS

CHAPTER ONE

WHAT IS WHITE PRIVILEGE?

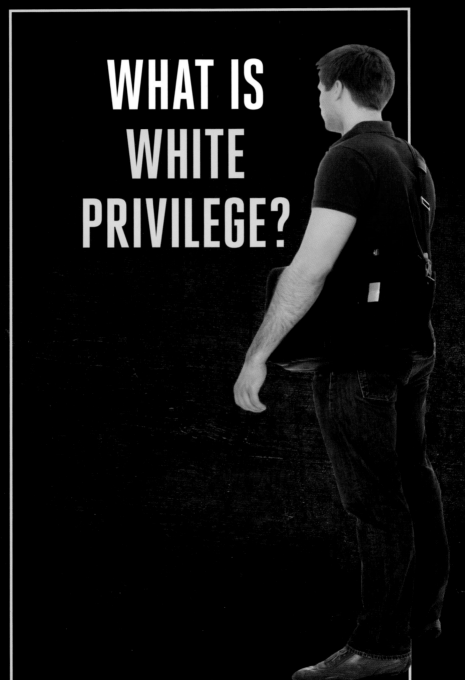

The concept of white privilege can be understood through an analogy. Imagine a steep, snow-covered mountain. Two climbers are racing to be the first to its summit. One climber lives right at the base of the mountain and starts his climb at sunrise. The air is brisk, but he is well equipped with a warm winter jacket and pants. He has gloves and shoes made for technical climbing. A second climber lives a couple of miles away and must walk this distance before she can start the climb. She dresses in layers of sweaters and wears heavy mittens and hand-me-down boots that fit pretty well but not perfectly.

After making it through a difficult pass, the first climber is met by a family friend who has hiked this section of trail many times. This friend shows the hiker an easier route. Meanwhile, the second hiker arrives at the mountain to begin her ascent. She comes across a group of men enjoying their morning coffee at the base of the mountain. To them, she is a potentially dangerous stranger, so they do not tell her about the easier route. Instead, she follows a path that takes her an hour off course.

The first hiker keeps climbing, scaling a rock face. He has had climbing lessons and owns a harness, so this climb is difficult but manageable. The second climber

In the climbing analogy, some hikers have assistance in scaling the peak, while others are left on their own.

finds herself at a rock face, too. This rock face is on the western side of the mountain, which receives little sun. It is covered in ice. She does not have the proper equipment and struggles to scale the ice wall. Her mittens are warm, but they make it hard to grip the ice. Eventually, she makes it.

The first hiker stops to eat his lunch. It was packed by a family friend who runs a business creating healthy meals for hikers. The second hiker is tired from climbing the ice wall when it's time for lunch. She's already behind, so she can't stop and rest. She chews on the beef jerky she got at the corner store while she scrambles to catch up with the first hiker.

The first hiker continues up the steep slope using hiking poles to steady his way. The second hiker has to scramble on her hands and knees. Her mittens and boots were not made for mountain climbing, so her fingers and toes are numb by now. Sometimes she slips and falls. As she climbs, rocks loosened by the first climber tumble down toward her, and she must dodge out of the way.

The first climber reaches the final stretch. It is a steep, treeless pass, and it is a huge struggle to reach the top. He collapses with exhaustion, but he makes it to the summit. The second hiker is still far behind. She has frostbite because she did not have gear as good as that of the first hiker. Her beef jerky lunch didn't fill her up, and she is dizzy from hunger. She stumbles as she continues to scramble up the mountain. She still has far to go, but the setting sun will force her to stop.

The first hiker is celebrated for his success. He worked very hard, everyone declares, and he earned his place at the summit. Observers imply, though rarely state outright, that the second hiker did not work hard enough. Perhaps she did not want it as badly. Either way, it is clear to the observers that the first hiker was the stronger, more deserving mountaineer.

ADVANTAGES AND CHALLENGES

Did the first hiker work very hard? Absolutely. But so did the second. The first hiker had advantages that made his climb easier, such as living closer to the mountain, having a friend with experience, and owning the proper equipment. Yet the second hiker faced obstacles at every turn—obstacles she could not control. Both hikers faced challenges, but these challenges were not equal. So to get to the same peak, the second hiker would need to overcome many more challenges.

White privilege works the same way. White people, because of their perceived race, are born with opportunities and advantages, while people of color often

Daily instances of discrimination, even when subtle, contribute to the overall presence of white privilege in society.

THE BICYCLE ANALOGY

Jeremy Dowsett, a white pastor from Michigan, believes that riding his bike helped him to understand white privilege as a form of "systematic imbalance" similar to the way cars and trucks dominate bike riders on the road. On his bike, he experienced some instances of open hostility. Drivers yelled at him to get off the road or purposefully drove through puddles to splash him. Most of the challenges he faced, however, were not from intentional hostility. Rather, drivers following the rules of the road were unintentionally dangerous to bikers. When a big rig truck passed him, the truck's wheels sprayed gravel over him. The truck driver probably didn't intend to spray Dowsett with gravel. He might not have even realized he was doing it. In this system, bike riders are at a dangerous disadvantage. Dowsett states, "I can imagine that for people of color life in a white-majority context feels a bit like being on a bicycle in midst of traffic. They have the right to be on the road, and laws on the books to make it equitable, but that doesn't change the fact that they are on a bike in a world made for cars."[1]

have hurdles thrown in their way. In Debby Irving's 2014 book, *Waking Up White and Finding Myself in the Story of Race*, she refers to this phenomenon as head winds and tail winds. While white people have a strong tail wind behind them blowing them forward, people of color are walking into a head wind and being pushed back. Without doing any extra work, the white person ends up with a significant benefit.

These metaphors—the mountain climbers, head winds, and tail winds— explain the subtle way white people are given advantages, both large and small, throughout their daily lives. White people may or may not intend to benefit from this system of advantages and disadvantages. In fact, to many white people, these advantages are so common that they take them for granted. They even become invisible. By not acknowledging the advantages, however, people credit the successes of white people to their hard work and natural abilities. By the same reasoning, failing to acknowledge the hurdles people of color face results in the assumption they have not succeeded because they have not tried hard enough. This is the legacy of white privilege.

White privilege plays out every day, in ways large and small. In the essay in which she first coined the term *white privilege*, Peggy McIntosh made a list of ways her life is made easier by being white. Some of these seem trivial, such as being able to find a plastic bandage that matches her skin tone. Some are more profound, such as seeing her story represented in the history books assigned at school. These advantages are so common that white people may not even notice them. Conversely, seeing unearned advantages go to white people again and again can be painful for people of color.

"As a white person, I realized I had been taught about racism as something that puts others at a disadvantage, but had been taught not to see one of its corollary aspects, white privilege, which puts me at an advantage."[2]

—Peggy McIntosh

W. E. B. Du Bois recognized that living in the United States gave white people advantages regardless of their financial status.

While the term *white privilege* may seem relatively new, the idea of race-based privilege has been around for nearly a century. The African American writer W. E. B. Du Bois wrote in the 1930s about how poor white people received a "psychological wage" that allowed them to feel superior to poor black people.[3] This is not a financial wage, but societal currency. Later, during the civil rights era of the 1960s, activists used the phrase *white-skin privilege* to talk about the advantages that come with being white in American society. McIntosh published her essays on white privilege in the late 1980s, and use of the term has risen steadily and sharply since then. More recently, scholars such as Beverly Daniel Tatum have continued to explore these themes. Tatum's 1997 book, *Why Are All the Black Kids Sitting Together in the Cafeteria?*, discusses how racism affects everyone in society. It also outlines ways in which racism can be overcome.

The concept of white privilege is less about one individual's specific advantages and more about the systemic underpinnings that allow white privilege to occur and to continue. White privilege is part of a larger system in which white people in general are given advantages over people of color. Understanding that system is key to understanding white privilege.

| DISCUSSION STARTERS |

- In the example of the mountain climber, what advantages did the first climber have over the second? What obstacles did the second climber face that the first did not? How might these be similar to everyday life scenarios?

- There are many different types of privilege. Can you think of some that aren't race based?

CHAPTER TWO

WHAT DOES IT MEAN TO BE WHITE?

There is no biological or genetic basis for race. In 2003, the Human Genome Project finished mapping out all the genes for humans as a species. Since then, scientists have been studying that data, with some trying to measure a quantifiable genetic difference between races. As it turns out, there is really not much of a difference from race to race. Traits that are typically used to classify races, such as skin color and eye color, are controlled by a very small number of genes. Humans as a whole have 99.9 percent genetic similarity.[1] There is more genetic variability within races than between them.

If race is not grounded in biology or genetics, but rather in perception, then who gets to be counted as white? This might seem obvious—people are white if they have white skin—but this has not always been the case. Groups of people now considered to be white were once deemed to be of a different race entirely from the white ruling class. In this way, who is considered white is a question of power. White people of power determine who is a part of their in-group, thereby giving those people a share of the power and the privilege of whiteness.

RACE AS A SOCIAL CONSTRUCT

In the 1600s, white landowners in the Jamestown Colony of Virginia faced a variety of threats. They feared uprisings from several groups, including local Native American populations such as the Doegs, Susquehannocks, and Occaneechi. Growing plantations used more and more enslaved people to do their labor, and there had been minor slave rebellions. Landowners also feared rebellions from white indentured servants who lived in poverty. Enslaved black people and white indentured servants saw one another as equals, sharing the same struggles.

The anger of poor white people in the Jamestown Colony toward wealthy landowners would later be redirected toward other races.

Sometimes these two groups plotted together to rebel against the wealthy landowners.

As the colony grew, however, these two groups grew to despise one another. Some historians believe this was by design, stemming from the circumstances of Bacon's Rebellion. William Berkeley, the governor of Jamestown, and Nathaniel Bacon, a wealthy resident from England, disagreed about how to deal with these perceived threats, particularly those from American Indian populations. Berkeley thought it was wisest to be friendly to those groups that were friendly to settlers or risk war with all the nations. Bacon believed all American Indians were dangerous. At the same time, locals with small farms were becoming discontented as they struggled with low prices for their crops and high taxes. Bacon recognized this anger and worked to redirect it as fear of local American Indians. Channeling fear and anger, Bacon amassed an army of poor farmers, white indentured servants, and enslaved black people. This group raided Indian territories and challenged Berkeley himself.

The rebellion never fully succeeded, but what it did demonstrate was that poor people of different ethnicities would come together to fight. That was a real threat to those in power. So the wealthy plantation owners left in power made several decisions. First, historians believe that this fear played a part in speeding up the shift away from indentured servitude toward race-based slavery. Second, the plantation owners realized that American Indians could be shaped into a common enemy of all white people. If poor white servants saw Native people as the source of their troubles, their attention and anger would not be directed toward the plantation owners.

The elites also realized they were safest if their enemies were divided rather than united. Rich whites and poor whites joined together in white populism, a belief that they had more in common with one another than with American Indians and enslaved black people. This feeling was supported by slave

"RACE IS THE CHILD OF RACISM"

Black author Ta-Nehisi Coates wrote *Between the World and Me* as a letter to his son. In the book, Coates questions the assertion that racism is the natural outcome of seeing race as an absolute. Instead, Coates flips this idea on its head and says that it is racism that led to the construct of race: "Americans believe in a reality of 'race' as a defined, indubitable feature of the natural world. Racism—the need to ascribe bone-deep features to people and then humiliate, reduce, and destroy them—inevitably follows from this inalterable condition. In this way, racism is rendered as the innocent daughter of Mother Nature, and one is left to deplore the Middle Passage or the Trail of Tears the way one deplores an earthquake, a tornado, or any other phenomenon that can be cast as beyond the handiwork of men. But race is the child of racism, not the father."[2]

By the late 1800s, the Irish community had largely been accepted as white, freely marching in Saint Patrick's Day parades in New York.

codes, laws that legalized unequal treatment of whites and blacks.

EARNING THEIR WHITENESS

In the 1840s, a potato blight in Ireland led to a mass emigration to the United States. When the Irish immigrants first arrived, Americans of English and Dutch descent saw them as inferior. The Irish did not have dark skin, but they were also not considered to be white. In the popular culture of the time, they were categorized

as lazy and often drunk. When Irish immigrants arrived, they quickly went after the low-wage, manual labor jobs that had traditionally been held by African Americans. The two groups competed for the same work. Irish immigrants settled primarily in cities. In contrast, many African Americans lived in rural areas at this time. Irish immigrants formed unions and became politically influential. The Democratic Party recognized this size and power and worked to appeal to the Irish. It did so by presenting a world view in which government was created by and for white men. To maintain its own status and power, the Democratic leadership worked to bring Irish immigrants into the party using white supremacy. Similar to Bacon's Rebellion, the Irish immigrants were persuaded to act in the interests of a race-based group—white people—rather than the working class. Some Irish immigrants aligned themselves with anti-abolitionists in the 1860s because fewer free black people meant less competition for paying jobs. Integrating the Irish ethnicity into the white race had two benefits: first, it increased the political power of wealthy white Democrats, and

RACE AND THE US CENSUS

Every ten years, the US Census tallies up the US population. Up until 1960, census takers would assign respondents a race. Afterward, respondents could choose their own racial identification, and starting in 2000, respondents were able to choose more than one race. Over the years, the categories for race have changed:

- 1790: Free white males, Free white females, All other free persons, Slaves

- 1890: White, Black, Mulatto, Quadroon, Octoroon, Indian, Chinese, Japanese

- 1990: White, Black or Negro, Aleut, Eskimo, Indian (American), Chinese, Japanese, Filipino, Korean, Asian Indian, Vietnamese, Hawaiian, Samoan, Guamanian, Other Asian or Pacific Islander, Mexican/Mexican American/Chicano, Puerto Rican, Cuban, Other Spanish/Hispanic, Other race

second, it served to keep African Americans in the position of being dominated.

Similar stories happened with Italian and Greek immigrants. While they were not initially welcomed into the white class, shifting power structures allowed them to work their way in. Whiteness, then, is more than skin color. It is a means to exert power over other people.

The treatment of immigrants during the 1800s shows the way the definition of whiteness has shifted over time. Some of this shift is the process of assimilation away from a foreign culture and into the dominant white, US culture, but it is important to remember that this process can be driven by power struggles. Conferring white status on a group is a means of giving that group power and, to a certain extent, protection.

| DISCUSSION STARTERS |

- What does it mean to say that race is a social construct?

- Look at the lists of categories of race used in the US Census. What can that tell you about changing perceptions of race in America?

- What do you think Coates means when he says that "race is the child of racism, not the father?"

WHITE
SUPREMACY

In order for there to be racism, groupings of people must be perceived as significantly different. But difference is not enough. One group must be considered superior. In the United States, it is whites who are seen as superior. This system is known as white supremacy, and it is at the root of white privilege. White supremacy is racial domination by whites. Different systems of supremacy are evident in different cultures worldwide. For example, the caste system in India privileges some groups over others. In Japan, the Burakumin is a group of people at the bottom of the social hierarchy. They have been the target of extreme discrimination.

THE LEGAL HISTORY OF WHITE SUPREMACY

White supremacy began in the United States before the country was even founded. The story of European settlement in America is one of conquest, often bloody and deadly. Colonists justified this violence by defining American Indians as wild and savage—an example of overt racism. The settlers saw no problem with taking Native lands. The logic of white supremacy meant that white colonizers saw this land as their right. This attitude continued as the colonies became the United States. As settlers expanded westward throughout the 1800s,

Generations of enslavement had lasting effects on African Americans, even long after the practice was outlawed.

the term *Manifest Destiny* was used to describe their movement onto American Indian land. This term was coined by John O'Sullivan in 1845 and described the belief that European American expansion was not only destined, but part of a duty to God.

Colonization is just one form of white supremacy evident in American history. Slavery was legal in the United States until 1865. Under this system, people who were enslaved were not treated as human beings; they were considered property. In fact, whether slaves should be counted as people was a big debate during the writing of the US Constitution. The Three-Fifths Compromise called for an enslaved person to be counted as three-fifths of a person when counting state populations for purposes of taxes and representation in the federal government.

The end of the American Civil War (1861–1865) brought about legal changes to government-sponsored white supremacy. Within five years, the US Congress passed three amendments to the Constitution. The Thirteenth Amendment abolished slavery in the United States. The Fourteenth Amendment granted citizenship to everyone who was born or naturalized in the United States, including people who had been enslaved. This meant that former slaves were supposed to have the same rights and protections as all other citizens. The Fifteenth Amendment stated that voting laws could not discriminate based on race or on a man's status as a former slave (at this point, women could not yet vote). Despite these amendments, African Americans continued to face legal discrimination.

Racist lawmakers found ways to circumvent the new federal laws. For example, while the Fifteenth Amendment was meant to prevent voting rights discrimination, local and state legislatures found ways around the rule. The amendment states that no race can be targeted by voting restrictions, so many former slave states instead imposed poll taxes or tests. Many former slaves could not afford to pay the tax. Voter registration officials could choose how to administer the tests, so they could give the easiest questions to white

The Fifteenth Amendment was meant to ensure African Americans could vote, but in reality many found obstacles in the way of casting a ballot.

citizens but require black citizens to answer the most difficult questions or to answer many questions in a very short amount of time. In this way, the laws effectively discriminated against freed slaves and other black citizens.

Lawmakers also passed legislation limiting the rights of African Americans. After the Civil War ended, many Southern states passed Black Codes. These laws affected African Americans only and restricted several rights, including those regarding marriage and property ownership. In addition, African Americans could not testify against white people in court, serve on juries, or vote. These laws gave rise to the Jim Crow era, when laws made the difference in treatment between black and white people not merely allowable, but required by law. Many states passed laws that did not allow mixed-race marriages. The intent of these antimiscegenation laws was to maintain racial purity. Although these laws were deemed unconstitutional in 1967 with the Supreme Court ruling in *Loving v. Virginia*, such relationships remain stigmatized in American culture. White supremacist groups such as the Ku Klux Klan (KKK) used lynching as punishment when they believed that people of color crossed social boundaries.

The Supreme Court's 1896 decision in *Plessy v. Ferguson* allowed public places to be segregated if facilities for white and black people were equal. The law permitted segregation in theaters, drinking fountains, buses, and countless other areas. In reality, the quality of the separated places was virtually never equal.

Federal and state governments excluded people from the legal privileges of whiteness through the so-called one-drop rules. Under

LEGAL TIMELINE

1787: The Three-Fifths Compromise is approved as part of the Constitutional Convention.

1790: The Naturalization Act of 1790 grants citizenship to white immigrants of good character.

1865: Slavery is abolished.

1896: *Plessy v. Ferguson* allows for separate public services for white and black people as long as the services are equal.

1954: *Brown v. Board of Education* finds the premise of separate but equal to be unconstitutional.

1967: *Loving v. Virginia* allows for interracial marriages.

these rules, a person with a single black ancestor—a single drop of "black blood"—was considered black. For decades after the end of slavery, this black status would affect a person's ability to find employment, housing, and education. The state of Louisiana finally repealed its racial classification law in 1983.

Although the Fourteenth Amendment promised all citizens equal rights and protections, minority groups needed to fight for equal access to education. *Brown v. Board of Education* stated that segregated schools were inherently unequal and that schools must be desegregated. However, racial segregation in schools is actually increasing. From 2000 to 2014, the percentage of racially isolated schools grew from 9 to 16

RACISM IN SCIENCE

The scientific community is not immune from racist ideology. African Americans were used as unwitting research subjects from 1932 to 1972 in the Tuskegee syphilis study. Six hundred black men were told they were being treated for *bad blood*, a local term for diseases including syphilis, anemia, and fatigue. Of these men, 399 had syphilis and 201 did not.[1] However, these men were not given the proper treatment for syphilis and were instead used to study the disease over time. These men were given free medical exams, meals, and burial insurance, but they were misled about the purpose of the study and the treatment they would receive. In 1972, the study was deemed unethical by a government advisory panel and stopped. In 1974, the participants won a class-action lawsuit, awarding them compensation for their mistreatment.

percent. An isolated school is one in which 75 percent or more of the students are from the same race or class.[2]

The legal implications of racism are not limited to targeting former slaves. White supremacy can be seen in US anti-immigration laws. For example, the Chinese Exclusion Act of 1882 banned Chinese immigration for ten years. It was renewed in 1892 for another decade. These laws devalued the familial and cultural connections of Asian Americans. In the 1920s, US Supreme Court cases denied people from Japan and India the ability to become citizens. Later, during World War II (1939–1945), Asian Americans would again be targeted when American citizens of Japanese descent were placed in internment camps. They were labeled as potential traitors and considered dangerous, based strictly on their heritage.

The same attitude is echoed in modern politics. In 2016, some mayors and governors, such as Maine's Governor Paul LePage, stated that they would no longer take part in the US government's resettlement program for Syrian refugees. LePage claimed that these refugees might be dangerous to the United States' security, despite a multiyear vetting process. He also said that they were a drain on his state's resources. In January 2017, President Donald Trump signed an executive order halting the

Thousands of Americans around the nation protested against Trump's executive order banning travel from seven majority-Muslim nations.

admission of refugees into the United States. The order also banned refugees from Syria indefinitely and banned entry into the United States from citizens of seven primarily Muslim countries. President Trump justified this order by saying the ban would make the nation safer. Such claims echo those made about previous immigrant groups, such as the Irish.

RACISM IN HOUSING

Racist housing practices kept blacks and whites apart, leading to more segregated communities. In the 1920s through the 1940s, this was done through racial covenants. Although it was illegal for cities or towns to make restrictions based on race, this was not the case for real estate boards and neighborhood associations. Participants in these boards and associations agreed not to sell their property to African Americans, thereby keeping their neighborhoods white. In 1926, the US Supreme Court ruled in *Corrigan v. Buckley* that this practice was acceptable. Private racial discrimination had been given legitimacy by the highest court in the United States.

In the 1930s, many Americans were suffering economic hardships caused by the Great Depression. The Federal Housing Administration worked to solve the home ownership crisis by insuring loans used for home mortgages. While this organization did do good work and helped many white people to purchase homes, its racist practices kept black people from the same benefit. It did so using a practice known as redlining. Neighborhoods with higher proportions of black citizens were deemed high risk, and loans for houses in these areas were hard to come by. These decisions were based solely on race, citing "inharmonious racial and nationality groups" to be as risky as "smoke, odors, and fog."[3] While redlining was outlawed in the 1960s and 1970s, racial discrimination continues when it comes to mortgage loans. For example, in 2014, a branch of Hudson City Savings Bank in Orange, New Jersey, approved 1,886 mortgage loans. Of those loans, only 25 were for black borrowers.[4]

White supremacy has directly influenced the first 150 years of American history, as is evidenced by examining America's changing laws. Laws that grew out of overt racism have set up a system that allows white people to dominate all sectors of life. Though many overtly racist laws have been repealed, their cumulative effect over the course of many decades continues to affect people today.

| DISCUSSION STARTERS |

- How have the laws of the United States reinforced racism in the country? When laws have outlawed racist practices, what are some examples of ways people have circumvented those laws?

- The impact of practices like redlining can still be seen today. Think of the area where you live: Can you see any evidence of the legal practices of the past?

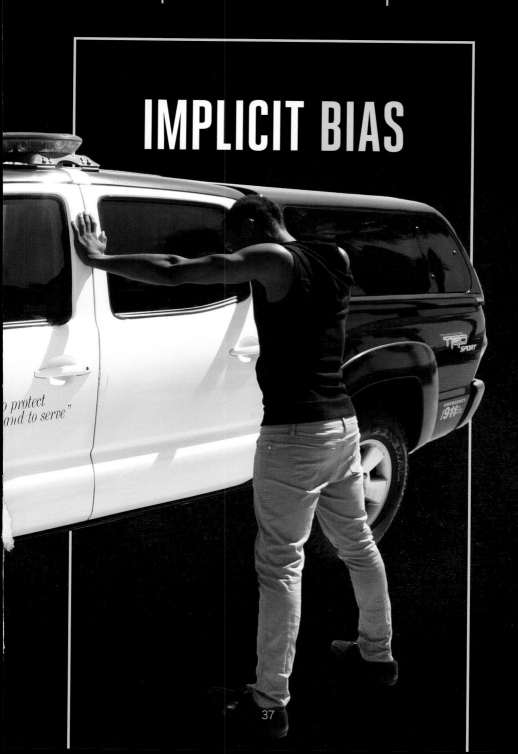

CHAPTER FOUR

IMPLICIT BIAS

In October 2016, African American high schooler Chase Coleman took a wrong turn while running a cross-country race. He wound up in the middle of the road in a downtown area. Coleman is autistic and nearly nonverbal, so he could not ask for help. When Martin MacDonald, a white man, saw Coleman, he assumed the teen was going to mug his wife, who was in the car with him. MacDonald got out of the car and approached Coleman, who did not respond. MacDonald, according to witness statements, then pushed Coleman to the ground.

What would make MacDonald assume that a boy wearing a cross-country uniform and a race number was a mugger? MacDonald told police that some African American youths had recently broken into his car. Why would MacDonald connect Coleman to the youths who had broken into his car? One explanation might be implicit bias.

Implicit bias is a bias in judgement that happens without conscious awareness. It is the result of the system of white supremacy that has been built into American law and culture since colonists first arrived in North America. Overt racism led to the creation of many of these laws, but the result is that the United States is systematically prejudiced in favor of white people. This is the root of white privilege. White supremacy is systemic, meaning that it infiltrates all aspects of culture and daily life. This can make it hard for some people to see and identify. In this way, prejudice or bias becomes implicit rather than explicit.

PROJECT IMPLICIT

Researchers at Harvard's Project Implicit have been studying the phenomenon of implicit bias. They make a distinction between explicit and implicit attitudes. An explicit attitude is one that you are aware of and are willing to report. If someone asks you about pizza, you likely have an opinion. Whether positive or negative, that is your explicit attitude about pizza. Implicit attitudes are ones that people are less aware of, or not aware of at all, and therefore cannot control. For example, perhaps you have never tried Ethiopian food, and someone asks you

DENYING IMPLICIT BIAS

Because implicit bias is not overt, it is easy for people to deny its existence. Whereas white people have the privilege of assuming their personal interactions with others are based on personality and character, minorities often wonder if their race played a role. Bijan Stephen, an African American writer from Brooklyn, writes about the role of implicit bias in his life in an online essay: "Is this why I didn't get the job? Is this why my lease application was denied? Is this why I got into college? Is this why this person keeps following me around the grocery store? And when you ask, you're looked at like you're crazy, met with denial—because it's always plausible, deniable."[1]

if you would like some. You might have an opinion about Ethiopian food, either positive or negative, that you can't quite explain. It could be based on implicit assumptions you have about the culture of Ethiopia, presumptions you make about the food, or other factors.

Along with implicit and explicit attitudes come implicit and explicit stereotypes. Stereotypes are beliefs about an entire group of people. Project Implicit gives the example that all police officers like doughnuts. As with attitudes, people may be aware of certain stereotypes, and they may even believe them. These are explicit stereotypes. Implicit stereotypes are ones that people may not even realize they believe.

When systemic structures of racism

IMPLICIT ATTITUDE TEST

How does Project Implicit test for implicit attitudes? The study offers a number of different tests relating to race, gender, sexuality, and more. During the test, a series of images and words flash onto the screen. Participants must quickly sort them. In the skin tone test, for example, the choices for sorting are good/bad and light skin/dark skin. In one round, participants must press one key when shown "bad" words or light-skinned faces and a different key when shown "good" words or dark-skinned faces. In another round, those associations are flipped. Participants must press one key when shown "good" words or light-skinned faces and a different key when shown "bad" words or dark-skinned faces. The study measures reaction times. A faster reaction time when "good" words are associated with light-skinned faces demonstrates an implicit bias for people with light skin tones.

meet the brain's natural instinct to categorize, implicit bias arises. With implicit bias, the brain makes a false connection and categorizes groups of people—for example, those who do not look white—as threats. Researchers with Project Implicit designed tests to reveal a person's implicit biases. Approximately 51 percent of people who take the Implicit Association Test show a moderate to strong bias for European Americans.[2]

THE EFFECTS OF BIAS

Implicit bias also shows up in hiring practices. Two résumés may be exactly the same, but when candidates have a white-sounding name, they are 50 percent more likely to receive an interview.[3] Implicit bias can also lead to common misconceptions. For example, most people on welfare are white, but there is a common belief that

Laws prohibit explicit bias in hiring practices, but many people still experience implicit bias.

welfare aids black people the most. Furthermore, people who incorrectly believe that most welfare recipients are black also believe the economic fate of those on welfare is caused by a "lack of effort on their part." On the other hand, those who accurately identify most welfare recipients as white ascribe their needs to "circumstances beyond their control."[4]

White supremacy, implicit bias, and white privilege are intertwined. Living in a system of white supremacy leads to implicit bias. This implicit bias is negative toward people of color. Implicit stereotypes for people of color are negative and assume the worst. On the other hand, implicit bias favors white people. It assumes good intentions on behalf of white people and gives them the benefit of the doubt. These positive associations with whiteness are at the root of white privilege. They mean that, given an identical set of circumstances, the outcome is likely to be better for a white person than for a person of color. To acknowledge white privilege, both the negative implicit bias against people of color and the positive implicit bias toward white people must be considered.

IMPLICIT BIAS IN LAW ENFORCEMENT

Implicit bias may play a role in how police officers respond to potentially dangerous situations. Their implicit biases can influence split-second decisions. When male police officers take part in first-person shooter simulations, they do better than average citizens at not shooting unarmed citizens. However, police officers were slower to select "don't shoot" for an unarmed black man than an unarmed white man, indicating that implicit bias influences them. The problem of implicit bias is exacerbated because approximately 88 percent of police officers are white.[5]

Simulations allow police officers to train for situations in which they must make quick decisions about the use of deadly force.

In the past several years, greater attention has been paid to the deaths of African Americans at the hands of police officers. The Black Lives Matter movement is one organization leading the charge to increase public awareness. Activists point to the disparity between how white people and minorities are treated in these types of situations. Being white tends to lead to fewer and less confrontational interactions with police. A white person in a white neighborhood is statistically less likely to be stopped by the police than a person of color. Once stopped, white people are less likely to have their vehicles searched than Hispanic or black people, even though police find more illegal materials when searching vehicles belonging to white people.

Interactions with police officers are less likely to end in violence or injury for white people than black people. There is limited data collected about police-involved shootings, but numbers from 2010 to

TAMIR RICE: A DEADLY CASE OF IMPLICIT BIAS

In November 2014, 12-year-old Tamir Rice was playing with a toy gun in a public park in Cleveland, Ohio. A witness called 911, stating that there was a person with a gun—a gun that looked as if it could be a toy. Still, when police arrived, they approached aggressively. One officer jumped out of the cruiser before it came to a stop. Seconds after arriving, that officer, Timothy Loehmann, fired his gun. Tamir Rice died. No police officer was ever charged in the boy's death.

2012 show that black teenaged men are killed by police at a rate 21 times higher than that of white teenaged men.[6] One answer for the disparities in the use of deadly force could be implicit bias.

RACE AND SENTENCING

Beyond the problem of police violence, white people also have an advantage in the American criminal justice system. Statistics about drug use and incarceration suggest white privilege plays a role in these areas as well. According to self-reports, almost five times as many white people use drugs as black people.[7] Logically, incarceration rates should reflect these proportions. There should be proportionally many more white people in jail for drug offenses. But this is not the case. African Americans are locked up for drug offenses at a rate that is ten times higher than that of white people.[8] Looking at it another way, black people make up just 12 percent of the nation's drug users but account for 38 percent of those arrested for drug offenses and 59 percent of those in state prisons for these offenses.[9] When it comes to sentencing, there is also a disparity. On average, white people convicted of a drug offense serve three fewer months than black people.[10]

Policies at the national, state, and even local level can influence the differing treatments of racial groups in

African American drivers are subjected to a disproportionate number of vehicle searches compared to white drivers.

the criminal justice system. Some favor policies that are touted as being tough on crime. New York City police officers have employed a program known as Stop and Frisk. This program allows the police to stop, question, and frisk individuals without probable cause, meaning officers do not have to have evidence suggesting a crime had taken place. Statistically, this practice affects more people of color than white people. Neighborhoods are targeted not because of high crime rates but because of the racial makeup of the area. The practice of Stop and Frisk has been challenged, and in 2013 New York City's policy was deemed unconstitutional by the US Supreme Court in *Floyd v. City of New York*. Despite this ruling, the practice has continued, although at a much lower rate. In the first half of 2016, New York City police officers completed fewer Stop and Frisk searches than in any year on record. Crime in New York City has continued to drop since the practice was reduced. Using Stop and Frisk does not translate to a lower crime rate. The policy does not make the general population any safer.

Implicit bias also contributes to unequal treatment in the criminal justice system. Research about implicit beliefs shows that people tend to think that people of color are more dangerous than white people. One form of white privilege is an assumption that white people are not dangerous. This implicit bias can show itself at any number of phases of the criminal justice system, including the point of arrest, the decision to prosecute, and sentencing. In these moments, the police officers, attorneys, and judges have varying degrees of choice in what happens. White people have opportunities to be set free at each of these stages if, because of their white skin, they are seen as less risky or their crimes as less serious.

| DISCUSSION STARTERS |

- Some scientists think that implicit bias is tied to the evolutionary need to quickly identify threats. How might such snap decisions have played a role in human evolution?

- Are there any ways in which implicit biases are helpful?

CHAPTER FIVE

WHITE PRIVILEGE IN EDUCATION

When Sylvia Mendez was a child in the 1940s, she wished her school had swings and monkey bars. The white school had a nice playground, and she wanted one, too. But school segregation was legal, as long as the schools provided equal education and services. So Sylvia had to attend a school designated for Hispanic students. School officials claimed the schools were equal, but Sylvia and her family knew this was not the case. Her parents fought for her to attend the white school, though they were more concerned about her educational opportunities than playground equipment. Sylvia's parents did not believe their daughter was getting an equal education, so in 1947 they filed a class-action lawsuit along with four other Latino families. Their case went to the Ninth US Circuit Court of Appeals, where they won and Sylvia was allowed to go to the white school. Seven years later, the US Supreme Court ruled in *Brown v. Board of Education* that separate schools were not equal, and schools had to be integrated.

Recent studies show that schools are still segregated along race and class lines. Today approximately 16 percent of students go to schools where 75 percent of the students are of the same race or class. In California, Sylvia Mendez points out, "Two schools that are named after my mother and father are 99 and 100 percent Latino, so what does that tell you? They fought and they won, so by law we cannot be segregated—that is called *de jure*—but what we have now is *de facto* segregation."[1] When schools are segregated by race, the schools that have mostly white students tend to have more math, science, and college prep courses than schools with mostly minority populations. The predominantly white schools also have fewer students who are held back, suspended, or expelled.

CULTURAL REPRESENTATION IN SCHOOLS

When white students walk into a school, they are likely to see teachers who look like them. They study textbooks written by white authors, which focus on white literature

In 2014, students in Colorado protested curriculum changes that would have de-emphasized historical protest movements by people of color.

and white history. This is one of the white privileges Peggy McIntosh lists in her essay. When US history is taught in schools, it tends to be from the perspective of white European Americans. In literature classes, the books studied tend to be by white authors. This is a daily example of white privilege in education: seeing oneself in the material studied.

Although there have been movements toward making the curriculum more diverse, the literature, history, art, and music studied are still largely produced by white people. Part of the problem is that this curriculum is not perceived as white. It is viewed as normal. When diverse topics are taught, they are often taught as something outside the regular curriculum. So the white privilege captured by the curriculum is that white culture is the norm, while everything else is outside of the norm. Critics often argue that changing the curriculum to be more diverse "waters down" what is taught, meaning the diverse texts are not as good or as rigorous as the traditional, white curriculum. But this claim itself is rooted in white supremacy. In a society that favors whiteness, white literature, history, art, and culture seem more important. However, this cannot be seen as an objective standard. Instead, it simply perpetuates the system of white supremacy.

Protesters have called upon governments to provide sufficient funding for high-quality public schools.

DISPARITIES IN RESOURCES

The United States is one of the only developed nations in which schools serving wealthier students have greater resources than schools serving lower-income students. This is because education in America is localized, and funding depends on local taxes. Richer cities and towns are able to raise more money in taxes for education. Richer areas tend to be whiter areas. Recent data show that approximately one-third of white students attend schools where the majority of students are low income, while nearly three-fourths of African American students do.[2] Since white students are more likely to be in higher-income schools, they receive a measurable benefit in their education. In the poorest 1,000 districts in the country, only 6.8 percent have students who meet or are above national averages.[3]

The difference in per-pupil expenditures is not simply a matter of the socioeconomic class of an area. Per-pupil spending has been tied to the racial makeup of a community, with one study finding that for every 10 percent increase in a school's minority population, the per-pupil spending went down by $75.[4] On average, white students in the United States have an extra $334 spent on them annually. A school with 90 percent white students spends, on average, $733 more per student than a school with a 90 percent minority population.[5]

The disparity in resources begins in early education and continues into the college years. White students are more likely to graduate from high school than minority students. Students of all races are about equally likely to start college after graduating from high school, but white students are more likely to graduate within six years.[6] White students are more likely to attend highly selective and well-funded colleges and universities.

Implicit bias affects students in the classroom as well. A white teacher is 30 percent less likely to predict a black student will complete a four-year college degree and 40 percent less likely to believe the student will graduate from high school as compared with the evaluations made by a black teacher.[7] Low expectations can negatively impact performance, putting black students at a disadvantage in school, while white students do not face that hurdle because of their race.

ZERO-TOLERANCE POLICIES

School discipline has been shown to vary along race lines. Students of color or students from non-English-speaking backgrounds have higher rates of disciplinary action, including suspension and expulsion, than their white peers. One culprit for this high rate is increasingly harsh discipline measures, including zero-tolerance policies.

Activist Marian Wright Edelman discusses how zero-tolerance policies can harm students.

Zero-tolerance policies were introduced as a way to reduce violence in schools. They require that certain actions at school not be tolerated. For example, the possession of guns was prohibited in 1994 by the Gun Free Schools Act. Punishment for breaking the rules is severe and does not consider context or any outside circumstances. These rules frequently do not take into account the severity of the offense. Under these policies, a five-year-old in Pennsylvania was suspended for bringing a toy ax as part of a Halloween costume.

While school violence and school shootings are very real problems, the situation is perhaps not as dire as people believe it to be. The rate of school violence has actually held steady or declined since the 1990s. Moreover, studies show these policies are often applied inconsistently. Rather than successfully curbing incidents of school violence, these policies have disproportionately affected students of color. Just as is the case with tough-on-crime laws, zero-tolerance policies tend to be used more often on minority students than white students. In the 2011–2012 school year, there were 49 million students in public schools. Of these, approximately 7 million were suspended. White students made up 51 percent of students, but accounted for just 40 percent of in-school suspensions. In general, as the punishment grows more severe, white students are less likely to be affected. In contrast, black students made up 16 percent of the student population but 32 percent of in-school suspensions.[8] African American students are almost three times more likely to be suspended than are white students.[9] This disproportionate rate of discipline problems for African Americans starts young, as early as preschool.

White students have greater rates of suspension for zero-tolerance rule breaking, such as bringing a gun or drugs to school, than African American students. But when the punishment for breaking a rule is discretionary, or left up to school officials to decide, African American students are more likely to be suspended. They are also more likely to be disciplined for subjective offenses, such as disrespect, which cannot be clearly defined. When the situation is ambiguous, white students are more often given the benefit of the doubt. On top of that, their punishments for minor rule violations, such

PRESCHOOL CHILDREN AND DISCIPLINE

According to a 2014 study by the US Department of Education Office for Civil Rights, suspension of preschool children is rare. Only 6 percent of school districts reported an out-of-school suspension for a preschool child.[10] However, the rate of suspension for white preschool children is disproportionately low, while the suspension rate for black children is disproportionately high.

as having a cell phone in class, tend to be less severe than those given to African American students. In other words, for committing a less serious act, African Americans are more severely punished.

The different treatment students of color receive in school can have lasting effects. When these students miss school, their academic achievements are affected. Missing class time means they are not learning the material. This leads to poor performance in school, which limits college selection or even results in a student not graduating. In turn, this makes it difficult to get good-paying jobs.

Why are white students treated differently than students of color? One factor may be teacher perceptions. Teachers, like everyone else, hold implicit biases. Some white teachers from different cultural backgrounds may perceive African American student behavior as hostile and violent. Just as with expectations of academic success, perceptions of student behavior vary with the race of the teacher. White teachers tend to rate black students as poor classroom citizens, whereas black teachers rate the behavior of these students more favorably than the behavior of white students. Because the majority of teachers are white, white students benefit from this implicit bias. Implicit bias can also lead teachers to discipline African American boys more severely because of deep-seated stereotypes of black males being more violent and dangerous. Teachers, particularly white teachers, may see African American male students as threats.

In the system of white supremacy, education works as both a tool and a product of systemic racism. White supremacy dictates a primarily white curriculum. White privilege means this is seen as normal rather than limited. This curriculum in turn reinforces the status quo in which white people have power over other groups. Likewise, for white students, schools are relatively safe spaces where they can succeed. For students of color, implicit bias and white supremacy lead to discipline and academic problems that hinder their success.

| DISCUSSION STARTERS |

- Why are segregated schools a problem?

- Think of the books you read for school; how diverse are they? Why do you think teachers choose to either include or not include books by diverse authors?

- When students are suspended or expelled, they fall further behind in school. What are some alternative consequences for rule breaking other than suspension or expulsion?

BOYCOTT

#OscarsSoWhite

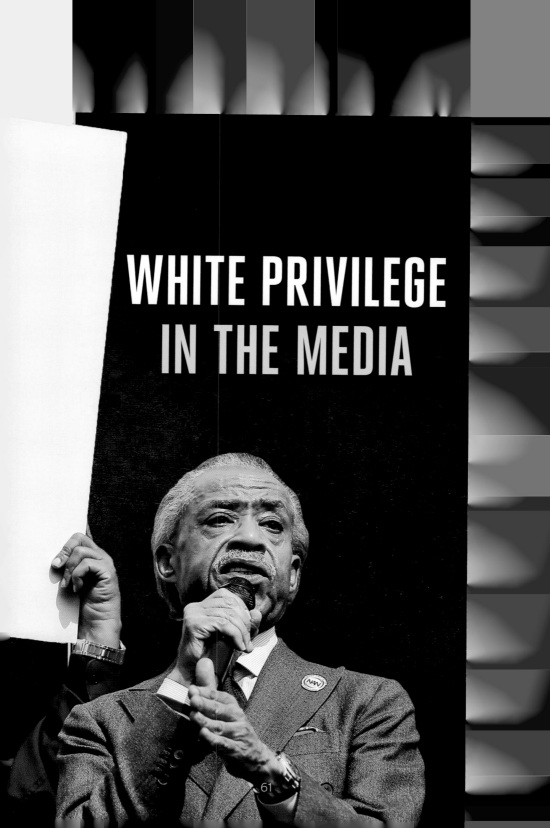

WHITE PRIVILEGE IN THE MEDIA

61

When the nominations for the 2016 Oscars were announced, critics noticed something about the nominees: whiteness. For the second year in a row, all 20 nominees in the acting categories were white. After the 2015 nominations, activist April Reign created the Twitter hashtag #OscarsSoWhite, and in 2016 the hashtag went viral again. Celebrities and activists tweeted their anger about the lack of diversity among the nominees.

After the backlash, the Academy of Motion Picture Arts and Sciences, the group that gives out the Oscars (also known as the Academy Awards), worked to diversify its membership. Members of the academy nominate and vote for the winners of the awards. They added 683 new members, 46 percent of them women and 41 percent people of color.[1] With these changes in place, the 2017 Oscar slate was far more diverse. Three of the films nominated for best film centered on black characters, and 7 of the 20 best actor nods went to people of color.[2]

At the same time, there was still a stunning lack of nominations for Asian and Hispanic actors and filmmakers. Only one Asian actor, Dev Patel in *Lion*, was nominated for an award. No Hispanic actors were nominated. This is historically consistent. From 2000 to 2017, 10 percent of acting nominations were for black actors, 3 percent for Hispanic actors, and only 1 percent for Asian actors.[3]

Why does representation in movies matter so much? One of the tools that supports and spreads the system of white supremacy is the media. Pop culture—television, movies, music, and books—is one area where racial stereotypes and structures are perpetuated. The research shows that people's levels of implicit bias can be influenced by messages received, either positive or negative. Many of the daily messages received about race come through the media, and these messages can train the brain to have negative or positive associations with different groups of people. When the message reinforces the stereotypes,

STEREOTYPES IN THE NEWS

White privilege shows up in our entertainment, but also in our news media. Stories of abducted white girls can dominate news coverage for weeks, months, or even years. But when a black child is missing, there may be no reporting at all. This phenomenon is known as Missing White Girl Syndrome.

In 2003, US soldiers in Iraq were ambushed. Among them were three women. Lori Piestewa, a Hopi woman and single mother, was killed. Two others, Shoshana Johnson and Jessica Lynch, were taken as prisoners. In the aftermath, news stories focused on Lynch. The Defense Department exaggerated her actions to make her seem like a greater hero. Johnson's role was minimized. The difference between the two women? Lynch is white, and Johnson is black. Lynch herself was upset by the different treatment the two women received.

implicit bias is observed at a higher level. Such stereotypes can have important real-world consequences in hiring discrimination and other areas. For this reason, it's important to examine the portrayal of whiteness and race in the media.

The Bunche Center for African American Studies at the University of California, Los Angeles, reports on diversity in Hollywood. Its findings show white people dominating film and television both in front of the camera and behind it. For example, moviegoers in 2013 were almost nine times more likely to see a white actor in the lead than a minority actor.[4] While the report shows a trend toward greater diversity in representation, the number of minority characters in film and television is far from representing the reality of the US population. In fact, minorities are underrepresented by a factor of two to one.[5] The same statistic holds true for directors of scripted shows on broadcast networks. At the same time, the shows and films that did have diverse casts were among the most successful, indicating that the viewing public would like to see more representation.

Sometimes characters who were written as minorities end up being played by white actors. This is known as whitewashing, and it has a long history in Hollywood. American Indian characters were portrayed by white

White actor Johnny Depp portrayed an American Indian character in the
2013 film *The Lone Ranger*.

The use of white actors, including Christian Bale, in *Exodus: Gods and Kings* drew criticism.

actors in recent films such as *Pan* and *The Lone Ranger*. In the film *Exodus: Gods and Kings*, Egyptians were played by white actors. Director Ridley Scott has been quoted as saying a nonwhite actor could not carry the film. Frequently, Asian and Asian American actors lose out on roles to white actors. Some recent examples include the films *Aloha*, *Doctor Strange*, and *Ghost in the Shell*. The

latter is a live-action adaptation of a Japanese anime film. White actress Scarlett Johansson was cast as the lead. Explaining the decision, screenwriter Max Landis stated, "There are no A-list female Asian celebrities right now on an international level."[6] Film executives use this argument to justify their choices, but as the Hollywood diversity report shows, diverse films and television are successful.

CULTURAL
APPROPRIATION

During the Halloween season, store racks are filled with costumes of zombies, witches, princesses, and superheroes. Stores also carry costumes of Japanese geisha girls, American Indians, and Mexicans. Many see the latter costumes as examples of cultural appropriation. Cultural appropriation happens when a dominant culture co-opts or steals a cultural tradition from a minority group. Typically, costumes rely on stereotypes and not a full understanding of the culture. Students at Ohio State University started the We're a Culture, Not a Costume campaign to educate their fellow students about why such costumes are hurtful.

Hip-hop music is another area in which claims of cultural appropriation are often leveled. Miley Cyrus has been called out for cultural appropriation because of twerking and wearing dreadlocks. Rappers such as Macklemore and Iggy Azalea have been charged with profiting off of black music. Macklemore addressed the issue of privilege in his song "White Privilege II." He tangles directly with the way his race has led to his success by rapping, "But the one thing the American dream fails to mention / Is I was many steps ahead to begin with."[7] He goes on to talk directly about white supremacy and the ways being white helped his career.

Some people argue there are benefits to cultural appropriation. Cultural sharing can lead to greater understanding. Others think that sometimes cultures are meant to spread. For example, in defending Iggy

Azalea, the rapper Questlove said, "We as black people have to come to grips that hip-hop is a contagious culture."[8] Still, critics of cultural appropriation point out that when whites earn more money and acclaim than the black originators of an art form, the inequalities should be recognized.

Macklemore, a successful white artist, has rapped about white privilege in his music.

WINDOWS, MIRRORS, AND SLIDING GLASS DOORS

Recent research suggests that reading novels can increase a person's empathy. Fiction readers are better able to understand what others are thinking and feeling. Rudine Sims Bishop describes the relationship between reading and empathy this way: "Books are sometimes windows, offering views of worlds that may be real or imagined, familiar or strange. These windows are also sliding glass doors, and readers have only to walk through in imagination to become part of whatever world has been created or recreated by the author. When lighting conditions are just right, however, a window can also be a mirror. Literature transforms human experience and reflects it back to us, and in that reflection we can see our own lives and experiences as part of the larger human experience. Reading, then, becomes a means of self-affirmation, and readers often seek their mirrors in books."[9]

REPRESENTATION IN LITERATURE

The problem of representation is also present in literature. Starting in 1985, the Cooperative Children's Book Center (CCBC) at the University of Wisconsin–Madison School of Education began tracking representation in books written for children. It studied those written and/or illustrated by African Americans. Over time it expanded its research to other minority groups. Books for children by and about minorities are limited in number and make up only a small portion of all books published. In 2015, the CCBC received 3,200 books from US publishers. Of these, just 10 percent were by minority authors and 14 percent centered on minority characters.[10]

Book critic and scholar Rudine Sims Bishop uses the metaphor of books as windows and mirrors. Books can offer readers a chance to see a new world through a window and their own world reflected back to them as in a mirror. For white readers, most books function as mirrors. White readers miss out on a window to other cultures, which Bishop feels could help groups to better understand one another. Most of popular culture functions in this way. White people often see themselves reflected back, while minorities rarely do.

| DISCUSSION STARTERS |

- Imagine you are casting a movie. What role should race play in your casting decisions? Should you be race blind or should race be a key factor?

- If people do not see themselves reflected in popular culture or see themselves misrepresented, how do you think that changes their self-perception?

- If you do not know anybody of a particular race, how would you know if the portrayals of that group were authentic or not?

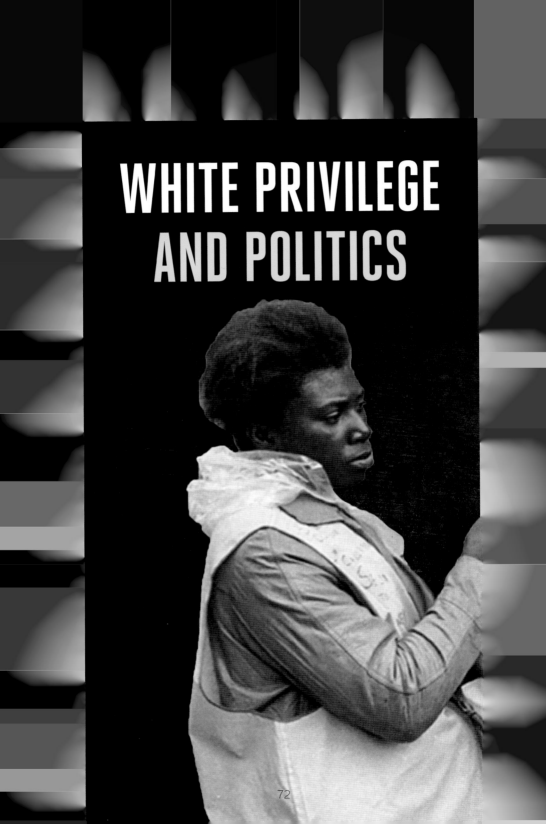

WHITE PRIVILEGE
AND POLITICS

Voting is often seen as a fundamental right of US citizenship. However, in the early days of the union, the question of who had the right to vote was so controversial that voting rights were not included in the Constitution or the Bill of Rights. Rather than agreeing on federal standards, each state had its own set of laws about who could vote. Some states required that people own property. Other states had more open voting laws and even allowed women and free blacks to vote. Black residents of Maine, New Hampshire, Vermont, Massachusetts, and Rhode Island could vote before the end of slavery. In New York, black citizens with at least $250 in property could vote. But such a restriction was not placed on white voters.[1]

After the Civil War, Congress ratified the Fifteenth Amendment, which stated that the "right of citizens of the United States to vote shall not be denied or abridged by the United States or by any state on account of race, color, or previous condition of servitude."[2] While the language of the amendment means there can be no racial discrimination, the intent of the law was to give African Americans the right to vote.

Unfortunately, the amendment did not have its intended effect for long. Up until the 1890s, newly

President Lyndon B. Johnson signed the Voting Rights Act on August 6, 1965.

emancipated African Americans took advantage of their new right to vote. Nearly 2,000 African Americans were elected to office during this time period.[3] All the while, black voters faced resistance and intimidation. In the 1890s, this resistance became more formal as poll taxes, literacy tests, and other policies kept African Americans from voting. In the South, when black people tried to register to vote, they might be arrested, beaten, or even killed. As late as 1965, only 7 percent of African Americans in Mississippi were registered to vote.[4]

The Voting Rights Act of 1965 was a response to these unfair practices. It prohibited any voter discrimination based on race. It also specifically outlawed any test as a requirement for voting. Other provisions of the bill were more complicated and placed special requirements on jurisdictions found to have racially biased voting laws in the past. This oversight was meant to prevent new, racially biased laws. This part of the law, known as section 4b, was struck down in 2013 in the US Supreme Court case *Shelby County v. Holder.*

VOTER DISENFRANCHISEMENT

Since that time, a number of new voting laws have emerged. These laws tend to have little effect on the ability of white people to vote. That is not the case for minority voters. One example is voter ID laws. Proponents of these laws believe they help to prevent voter fraud. Critics say minorities are less likely to have government-issued IDs and are less likely to have the documentation necessary

VOTER SUPPRESSION AND THE 2016 ELECTION

The 2016 election was the first presidential election without the full protection of the Voting Rights Act. Fourteen states had new laws that affected voting. Some people believe new voter ID laws, reduced funding for early voting, and more difficult voter registration disenfranchised many voters and could have affected the outcome of the election. On election day, there were 868 fewer polling places nationwide than in 2012.[5] The cuts were primarily in states that had a history of voter discrimination. Minority voter turnout was lower in the 2016 election than it was in 2008 and 2012.

to get IDs. There is also a cost of time and money to get IDs that may present a barrier to voting. For minorities, who are more likely living in poverty, the cost of an ID might be too high. Former attorney general Eric Holder argued that the cost of getting proper ID is a new version of a poll tax.

Critics believe voter ID laws act as a deterrent and keep minority voters away from the polls even if they are qualified and registered to vote. In one Texas election, 12.8 percent of registered voters who did not vote said they didn't vote because they believed they didn't have proper ID. However, only 2.7 percent of those nonvoters actually lacked the proper ID.[6]

Critics have also questioned why some forms of ID are accepted while others are not. For example, in Texas, a voter can use his or her concealed carry permit as identification, but not a student ID from a state university. The process of getting a proper ID to vote becomes so difficult that some voters give up. Voting statistics seem to support this claim. Researchers at the University of California at San Diego found steep drop-offs in minority voting between 2008 and 2012 in states with strict voter ID laws.

Laws that are explicitly race-based are not likely to hold up in court. For example, a Hawaiian law that

TIMELINE OF VOTING RIGHTS

- 1870: The Fifteenth Amendment prohibits racial discrimination in voting.
- 1903: In *Giles v. Harris* and *James v. Bowman,* the Supreme Court upholds policies that disenfranchise black voters.
- 1920: The Nineteenth Amendment gives voting rights to women.
- 1944: In *Smith v. Allwright,* the Supreme Court finds the practice of prohibiting African Americans from voting in primaries to be unconstitutional.
- 1950: South Carolina is the first state to pass a voter ID law. Poll monitors could request but not require some form of ID. The ID did not need to have a photo.
- 1965: The Voting Rights Act of 1965 becomes law.
- 2005: The Commission on Federal Election Reform recommends voter ID laws be passed.
- 2008: Indiana and Georgia laws that require an ID to vote go into effect.

stated that only native Hawaiians could vote on certain issues was deemed unconstitutional in 2000. However, the case is not so clear if the law is not explicitly based on race. Challengers must show how the law causes disenfranchisement based on race. This can be much harder to prove. So when Indiana's voter ID law was challenged in 2008, the Supreme Court ruled this law did not violate the Voting Rights Act. Although the plaintiffs successfully showed voter fraud was minimal, making the law unnecessary, they could not prove the law was racially motivated.

POLITICAL POSITIONS OF POWER

Rules regarding felons can also disproportionately affect people of color. People who have been convicted of certain crimes are banned from voting. The time between conviction and restoration of rights varies from state to state, with some states, such as Mississippi, permanently preventing voting for people convicted of certain crimes. Since minorities are convicted of crimes at higher rates than white citizens, such felon voter laws affect them disproportionately.

In Alabama, the 1901 constitution prevents anyone who has committed a crime "involving moral turpitude" from voting.[7] *Turpitude* is an adjective or label to describe something truly wicked. The word's application, of course, is subjective. The crimes that were deemed "involving moral turpitude" were those more frequently committed by African Americans.[8] The head of Alabama's 1901 constitutional convention declared that the purpose of this rule was to "establish white supremacy in this state."[9] Since this language is explicitly race-based, this law was deemed unconstitutional in 1985. The phrase *moral turpitude* was declared to be a violation of the Fourteenth Amendment, which guarantees equal rights and privileges. In 1996, though, the language was reinstated by the state legislature. Decisions about

FLINT, MICHIGAN

One impact of disenfranchisement is a lack of power in the political system. This can have an impact on the day-to-day decisions of government. For example, funding for water and sewer projects has been on the decline. Reports show that poorer cities have been disproportionately affected. One such city is Flint, Michigan. In 2014, city officials decided to change the source of drinking water for the city. City residents immediately reported that the water looked, smelled, and tasted bad. Their complaints were dismissed. After a few months, scientists discovered *E. coli* bacteria and human waste in the water, as well as high lead levels. High lead levels are dangerous, especially to pregnant women and children. Ingesting lead can lead to learning disabilities and behavioral problems.

Some people believe the Flint water crisis would never have happened had the city been predominantly white. Of Flint's population, 41.5 percent fall below the poverty line and 56.6 percent are African American.[11]

whether a convict may vote are left up to voting officials who control the voter lists. In 2016, nearly 15 percent of otherwise eligible black voters could not register to vote.[10]

WHITE OVERREPRESENTATION IN GOVERNMENT

The majority of lawmakers in the United States are white. In 2015, the National Conference of State Legislatures reported on the racial and gender makeup of state legislatures, the state-level governing bodies. The legislators were mostly white men. While African American representation grew from 2 percent in 1971 to 9 percent in 2015,

Whites have long been overrepresented in positions of power within the US government.

that number is still shy of 13 percent—the representation of African Americans in the general population. Hispanic lawmakers represent 5 percent of representatives, compared with 17 percent of the population.[12] Whites are also overrepresented at the national level. In 2015, 61 percent of the country was white, but 81 percent of representatives were.[13]

Why do whites hold such a large percentage of political offices? One reason is that white people, especially white men, run for office more often than people of color. Approximately 2 percent of Americans run for office. Whites make up 82 percent of these candidates.[14] People of color are elected at about the same rate they run. That is, when they do run, they tend to win. The barrier to representation seems to be at the candidacy stage.

Implicit bias and stereotypes influence potential candidates' perceptions of their chances of winning. White candidates are more likely to believe they can win. They have more role models in office and see themselves as having the qualifications to win. Minority candidates may perceive themselves as less likely to win.

THE IMPACT OF OVERREPRESENTATION

With a majority of white people in charge of legislation, the laws enacted tend to favor white people. A striking example can be seen in drug-sentencing laws. In the 1980s, crack cocaine ravaged segments of the black community. The legislative response was strict and punitive. In the mid-2010s, a heroin epidemic became apparent in many states. This time around, much of the response has been focused on treating addicts rather than imprisoning them.

Some people believe the difference is because crack cocaine was seen as a black problem, while heroin use is more widespread in affluent, white communities. Marc Mauer, the executive director of the Sentencing Project, stated, "When the perception of the user population is primarily people of color, then the response is to demonize and punish."[15]

DISCUSSION STARTERS

- Consider the pros and cons of voter ID laws. Do you think voter ID laws are helpful or hurtful for democracy?

- How does the overrepresentation of white people in Congress contribute to white supremacy?

- Do you think convicted criminals should lose their right to vote? Why or why not?

CHAPTER EIGHT

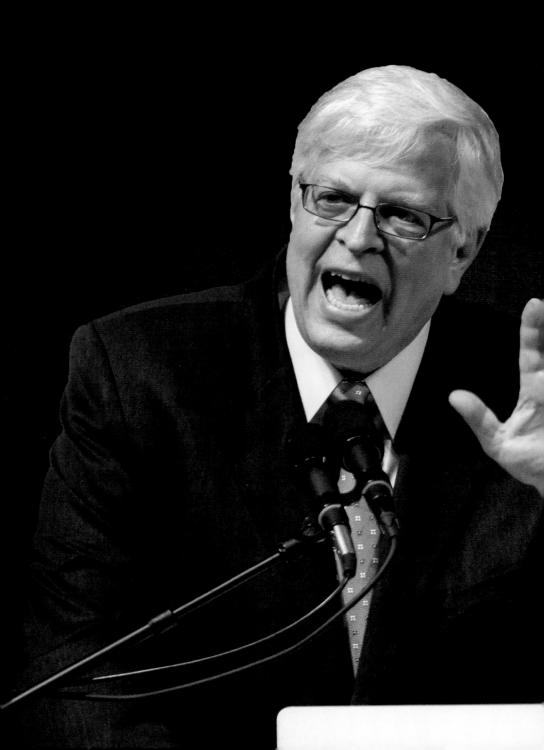

CRITIQUES OF WHITE PRIVILEGE

The most common critique of white privilege is that it does not actually exist. Detractors argue that factors other than race contribute to an individual's success. Being white, they argue, does not guarantee an advantage. Moreover, they argue, white privilege ignores personal responsibility. Conservatives argue that white privilege claims that white people are not at all responsible for their success. Conservative radio host Dennis Prager believes that the concept of white privilege negates the hard work white people might have put into their accomplishments. He writes, "There are simply too many variables other than race that determine individual success in America."[1] This critique misrepresents white privilege, arguing that white privilege allows only whiteness as a factor impacting advantages and disadvantages.

Critics specifically question whether race or class is the bigger form of privilege. Poor white people face many of the same challenges that poor people of color do. Gina Crosley-Corcoran, a white feminist blogger, wrote of how she struggled with the idea of white privilege—specifically Peggy McIntosh's list of privileges—for a long time. "When I first wrote about White Privilege years ago, I demanded to know why this White Woman felt that my experiences were the same as hers when no, my family most certainly could not rent housing '*in an area which we could afford and want to live.*'"[2] Crosley-Corcoran took issue with McIntosh's claim that being white meant you could live in any neighborhood you desired. Crosley-Corcoran's own experience growing up poor proved otherwise, and she questioned this and other class-based claims made in McIntosh's essay. However, scholarly analysis has shown that even the poorest whites have benefited from white privilege in some ways as a result of historical discrimination against their black neighbors in education, employment, housing, and other areas.

Crosley-Corcoran goes on to explain that people can be privileged in some ways but not in others. This is known as intersectionality. McIntosh is firm in her call for individuals to examine their own specific privileges. For example,

INTERSECTIONAL FEMINISM

Each person's identity is made up of different building blocks including race, gender, class, ethnicity, sexuality, and physical ability. Some aspects of your identity might give you privilege, while others may not. Feminists have been wrestling with the question of intersectionality for decades. Feminists who are also people of color have often felt that feminism has focused too much on the needs of white, middle-income women. They called for a more inclusive platform. The term *intersectional feminism* was coined by law professor Kimberlé Crenshaw to describe how feminism can be more inclusive of women of color.

she herself looks at other women in university positions and compares her own privileges with theirs.

Prager, however, believes that talking about white privilege is a way to cast black people as victims. He claims liberals have a political goal in highlighting racism. Minority groups have traditionally voted for Democrats since the 1930s. Prager and others argue that by making minorities victims, Democrats perpetuate a belief that people of color need protection from society and that Democrats are the ones most likely to provide that shield. Conservatives argue that discussing white privilege is a cynical way liberals court these voters.

There is also criticism that discussing white privilege re-centers the conversation on white people. In doing so, it again marginalizes the targets of racism: people of color. In particular, public confessions of one's own white privilege are controversial. When white people point out their own privileges, the purpose can seem to be less about self-criticism and more about self-congratulation. Writing in the *Washington Post*, academic Fredrik deBoer argued that these public confessions are really about pointing out how other white people have not yet awakened to their own self-privilege. Acknowledging one's own privilege does not necessarily lead to action that helps those affected by racism.

Since race is a social construct, some see this fact as a reason to ignore race and race-based discussion. They argue that society should be "color-blind" and see people as individuals, not as members of their race. Journalist and playwright David Marcus argues that "only when everyone views snap judgments about individuals based on race as the absurd equivalent of such judgments based on hair or eye color, will the great moral victory over bigotry be won."[3] The belief in white privilege, he implies, is as illogical and problematic as racism itself.

Many white people are uncomfortable with the notion of white supremacy. Most white people do not see themselves as racist and certainly do not see themselves as white supremacists. To many white people, white supremacy is synonymous with lynching, and a racist is a white person who uses the N-word. For many white people, the

DECLARATION OF WHITE PRIVILEGE

Writer Fredrik deBoer has argued that when white people confess their privilege, what they are really doing is congratulating themselves on their own enlightenment: "We're living in a time of broad awakening to the reality of deep, entrenched racial inequality. That's a great thing, but even the thought of being implicated in this system has caused anxiety in many white people, that some address by outdoing each other to be the loudest, most visible opponents of racial inequality."[4] Calling out their white privilege is a way to say they are one of the "good" white people who are aware of and opposed to racism.

COLOR BLINDNESS

Sometimes people will say, "I don't see color." What they mean by this is that they see the person before they see the person's race. This is known as color blindness. The intent of color blindness is to judge people by their character, not their skin color. Critics of color blindness argue that when we focus on individual relationships, we ignore the problem of systemic white supremacy. This in turn makes white people blind—not to race but instead to racism. Author Mychal Denzel Smith writes that color blindness leads people to believe that "racism is (a) matter of personal bigotry—racists hate people because of the color of their skin, or because they believe stereotypes about groups of people they've never met—not one of institutional discrimination and exploitation."[5]

term *racist* is reserved for people participating in extreme forms of racism. However, refusing to identify implicit bias and prejudice as racist is one way that white privilege is perpetuated. Just using the term *white supremacy* can cause some white people to back out of the conversation. They see themselves as "nice people" who are not racists.

INDIVIDUALS OR THE SYSTEM?

Finally, critics argue that white privilege examines individual privilege but not the system. Some take issue with McIntosh's focus on the individual. While McIntosh invites white people to examine their own individual privileges, she does not ask them to examine the underlying structure of white supremacy. Ignoring this underlying structure prevents antiracist action. This focus on the individual looks past the systemic issues that underpin white privilege.

For her part, McIntosh makes clear that not all white people experience the same white privileges. In her early essay, she compares her experiences to those of her coworkers who are women of color. Her list of white privileges are specific to her work, city, and experiences. For example, a white man might say that part of his white privilege is to be able to walk alone at night in his neighborhood without feeling afraid. McIntosh does not list this as one of her privileges, perhaps because as a woman she would not feel safe. Likewise, a white man who is gay or transgender might not share the privilege. Gender, levels of education, socioeconomic class, and other factors all play a role in any given white person's white privilege.

| DISCUSSION STARTERS |

- Which of the criticisms of white privilege seem to have the most merit to you?

- Can you think of other criticisms of white privilege?

- What are the benefits and drawbacks of being color-blind?

CHAPTER NINE

MOVING FORWARD

Having open conversations about race and privilege can help people recognize the issues that persist in America today.

CHANGING RACE RELATIONS

Writer Roxane Gay has written many essays about race relations in the United States. She notes that moving forward will require tough discussion and introspection. Although she questions whether such work is possible, she argues that not trying is not an option: "These conversations are always so tense, so painful. People are defensive. We want to believe we are good. To face the racisms and prejudices we carry forces us to recognize the ways in which we are imperfect. We have to be willing to accept our imperfections and we have to be willing to accept the imperfections of others. Is that possible on the scale required for change? . . . The alternative is silence, and silence is unacceptable."[3]

Because white privilege is often unrecognized by the people who benefit from it, the first step is to recognize the issue. Recent reports show that only approximately 25 percent of white Americans think white people have many advantages that people of color do not.[1] In contrast, nearly 66 percent of Americans of color believe this to be true.[2]

In order to bring white privilege to light, people can talk more about race and privilege. White people may be reluctant to have these conversations, but talking about it can bring groups together and can begin to bridge the gaps. By acknowledging white privilege, people will be able to more fully understand racial injustice and move toward greater equality.

One way to make these discussions more comfortable and fruitful is to examine racism and white privilege in terms of actions or consequences. Some activists advocate for talking about people's intentions and consequences instead of simply labeling people as racists. When people think about racism in terms of actions rather than unchangeable labels, they can choose to act in ways that oppose racism. That is, white people can identify their own white privilege and then resolve to act in ways that do not perpetuate this privilege.

In working to understand race and white privilege, some have chosen to explore the practice of treating whiteness as normal. Poet Claudia Rankine received a MacArthur Grant in 2016 and intends to use the money to form a center to study whiteness because "it's important that people begin to understand that

PRIVILEGE EXERCISES

Some schools and colleges do an exercise known as a Privilege Walk. This experiential activity is meant to help students understand privilege and intersectionality. Participants line up in a horizontal line in a gymnasium or other large space. Statements are read aloud and participants move forward or backward accordingly. For example, "If you can find Band-Aids at mainstream stores designed to blend in with or match your skin tone, take one step forward" or "If you have an invisible illness or disability, take one step back."[4] The goal is that participants will better understand their own privileges and the ways that privileges intersect.

whiteness is not inevitable, and that white dominance is not inevitable."[5] Her goal is to examine the role of whiteness and make it more visible.

EXAMINING EDUCATION

Some schools, such as those in California's San Francisco Bay Area, are turning away from out-of-school suspensions and moving toward new ways to deal with discipline issues, such as restorative justice. In restorative justice programs, students work to understand the underlying causes of their own actions. They must confront the victims of their crimes as part of the process. Restorative justice programs can also be a part of the criminal justice system. In a similar approach, some schools in Baltimore, Maryland, are trying meditation as a means of dealing with discipline problems.

There is also a profound diversity gap in schools. Nearly one-half of students are from racially diverse backgrounds, but as many as 80 percent of teachers are white.[6] This creates a cultural gap where white teachers might struggle to relate to their students of color. One way schools can increase teachers' cultural awareness is to implement culturally responsive teaching. This method connects curriculum with the personal experiences of students. Teachers work closely with students to better understand their cultural backgrounds and adapt their teaching styles accordingly.

TARGETING BIAS

Some researchers are looking at ways to target implicit bias directly. They are testing interventions with the Implicit Association Test. So far, the most successful way to reduce implicit bias has been for participants to first read passages in which a black person is their ally and a white person is causing harm. Presentations that ask participants to critically engage with cross-cultural connections are also effective in reducing implicit bias. This strategy also worked in a test that used a job hiring scenario: research participants who had a cross-cultural

WE NEED DIVERSE BOOKS

In 2014, BookCon, a large convention in the book industry, announced an all-star panel of children's authors. This panel also happened to be all-male and all-white. Authors Ellen Oh and Malinda Lo started an online discussion about their frustration surrounding the lack of diversity in children's literature. The two authors had discussed this many times before, and Oh decided to take action. From this conversation, the organization We Need Diverse Books was born. The group works to diversify children's publishing by highlighting diverse books and encouraging more diverse people to work in the industry. Author Corinne Duyvis created a hashtag, #OwnVoices, to highlight authors that contribute authentic voices that speak to their own experiences.

lecture chose a white candidate 56 percent of the time, compared with participants who saw a presentation about white American culture, who chose a white candidate 81 percent of the time.[7] This research suggests implicit bias and prejudice can be undermined, at least for short periods. It is possible to do this on one's own. Researchers at the University of North Carolina–Chapel Hill suggest that people think the word *safe* every time they see a black face. This trick could help to undermine deep-seated stereotypes.

In 2016, the US Department of Justice called for a more diverse police force and offered suggestions for how to bring that about. There is some anecdotal evidence that when antibias training is given to police officers, it positively influences their police work. More research might show this approach to be effective. The Las Vegas, Nevada, police department is trying to take implicit bias out of the equation as much as possible. Incidents of officer violence occurred most often after police chased suspects on foot. A new policy implemented around 2010 stated an officer could not physically restrain a suspect after a foot chase. If physical contact was needed, it had to be done by an officer not involved in the chase. The idea is that the officer pursuing the suspect would have his or her emotions amplified by adrenaline and thus be more likely

Some police departments have added antibias training to their educational programs.

to make a quick, biased decision. With the new policy, use of force has declined.

White privilege is part of a much larger system. It is rooted in the social construct of race, which itself is grounded in white supremacy. White supremacy leads to implicit bias, a form of racism that infiltrates most aspects of our day-to-day life, including our education and legal systems and our popular culture. These institutions both reflect and reinforce white privilege. Dismantling this system may seem an impossible task, but activists, educators, lawmakers, and others are all working toward greater understanding of implicit bias and white privilege.

ESSENTIAL
FACTS

SIGNIFICANT EVENTS

- In the 1930s, African American writer W. E. B. Du Bois described how poor white people receive a "psychological wage" that allows them to feel superior to poor black people.

- In the late 1980s, Peggy McIntosh published "White Privilege: Unpacking the Invisible Knapsack."

- The sequencing of the human genome in the early 2000s showed that neatly defined racial categories have little scientific basis. If there is little difference in the human genome, then the advantages that white people have must have a cultural basis.

KEY PLAYERS

- Peggy McIntosh coined the term *white privilege*.

- Kimberlé Crenshaw introduced the idea of intersectionality.

- In response to police violence, the Black Lives Matter movement has worked to counter white supremacy.

IMPACT ON SOCIETY

White privilege refers to the unearned privileges that white people receive every day because of their race. These might be simple things, such as being able to find "skin-toned" bandages that match their skin. Or they may be more serious, such as generally having positive interactions with law enforcement. The idea of white privilege was popularized by Peggy McIntosh. She examined her own privilege and came up with a list of ways whiteness helped her. Some people think white privilege does not really exist or that it re-centers the problem of racism on white people. Other people think understanding whiteness and white privilege is essential to understanding and dismantling racism.

QUOTE

"As a white person, I realized I had been taught about racism as something that puts others at a disadvantage, but had been taught not to see one of its corollary aspects, white privilege, which puts me at an advantage."

—*Peggy McIntosh*

GLOSSARY

CENSUS
An official counting of the people in a country, city, or town generally including age, race, and other demographic information.

EMANCIPATED
Freed from slavery.

INCARCERATION
The act of putting someone in prison or jail.

INTERNMENT
Confinement or imprisonment.

JURISDICTION
A political territory.

LYNCHING

The act of illegally killing a person through mob action.

MISCEGENATION

An offensive term for sexual relations or marriage between people of different races.

OVERT

Easily seen.

STATUS QUO

The way things are currently.

SUPREMACY

Having more power or authority.

SYSTEMIC

Part of an entire system.

ADDITIONAL RESOURCES

SELECTED BIBLIOGRAPHY

Coates, Ta-Nehisi. "What We Mean When We Say 'Race Is a Social Construct.'" *Atlantic*. Atlantic, 15 May 2013. Web. 23 Feb. 2017.

McIntosh, Peggy. "White Privilege: Unpacking the Invisible Knapsack." *National SEED Project on Inclusive Curriculum*. Wellesley College, 1989. Web. 23 Feb. 2017.

Nellis, Ashley. "The Color of Justice: Racial and Ethnic Disparity in State Prisons." *Sentencing Project*. Sentencing Project, 14 June 2016. Web. 23 Feb. 2017.

FURTHER READINGS

Bakshi, Kelly. *Roots of Racism*. Minneapolis, MN: Abdo, 2018. Print.

Edwards, Sue Bradford, and Duchess Harris, JD, PhD. *Black Lives Matter*. Minneapolis, MN: Abdo, 2016. Print.

WEBSITES

To learn more about Race in America, visit **abdobooklinks.com**. These links are routinely monitored and updated to provide the most current information available.

FOR MORE INFORMATION

For more information on this subject, contact or visit the following organizations:

THE AMERICAN CIVIL LIBERTIES UNION (ACLU)
25 Broad Street, 18th Floor
New York, NY 10004
212-549-2500
http://www.aclu.org

The ACLU fights to preserve the rights and freedoms of all Americans. Each state has its own affiliate that you can contact for more information.

THE NATIONAL CIVIL RIGHTS MUSEUM
450 Mulberry Street
Memphis, TN 38103
901-521-9699
http://www.civilrightsmuseum.org

Learn more about the civil rights movement at this museum in Tennessee. Visit its website for resources and activities.

SOURCE NOTES

CHAPTER 1. WHAT IS WHITE PRIVILEGE?

1. Jeremy Dowsett. "What Riding My Bike Has Taught Me about White Privilege." *Quartz*. Quartz, 29 Aug. 2014. Web. 16 Jan. 2017.

2. Peggy McIntosh. "White Privilege: Unpacking the Invisible Knapsack." *National SEED Project*. National SEED Project, 1989. Web. 13 Mar. 2017.

3. Joshua Rothman. "The Origins of 'Privilege.'" *New Yorker*. New Yorker, 12 May 2014. Web. 31 Oct. 2016.

CHAPTER 2. WHAT DOES IT MEAN TO BE WHITE?

1. "Race in a Genetic World." *Harvard* Magazine. Harvard Magazine, May–June 2008. Web. 18 Jan. 2017.

2. Ta-Nehisi Coates. *Between the World and Me*. New York: Spiegel & Grau, 2015. Print. 7.

CHAPTER 3. WHITE SUPREMACY

1. "The Tuskegee Timeline." *CDC*. CDC, 8 Dec. 2016. Web. 13 Mar. 2017.

2. George Toppo. "GAO Study: Segregation Worsening in US Schools." *USA Today*. USA Today, 17 May 2016. Web. 14 Nov. 2016.

3. "1920s–1948: Racially Restrictive Covenants." *Historical Shift from Explicit to Implicit Policies Affecting Housing Segregation in Eastern Massachusetts*. The Fair Housing Center of Greater Boston, n.d. Web. 23 Jan. 2017.

4. Rachel L. Swarns. "Biased Lending Evolves, and Blacks Face Trouble Getting Mortgages." *New York Times*. New York Times, 30 Oct. 2015. Web. 13 Mar. 2017.

CHAPTER 4. IMPLICIT BIAS

1. Bijan Stephen. "The Talk: How Black Parents Prepare Their Young Sons for Life in America." *Medium*. Medium, 20 Aug. 2014. Web. 14 Nov. 2016.

2. Chris Mooney. "The Science of Why Cops Shoot Young Black Men." *Mother Jones*. Mother Jones, 1 Dec. 2014. Web. 14 Nov. 2016.

3. Sally Kohn. "Eight Things Every White Person Should Know about White Privilege." *Daily Beast*. Daily Beast, 7 May 2014. Web. 1 Nov. 2016.

4. Ibid.

5. Matt Zapotsky. "The Surprising Ways the Justice Department Found to Help Diversify Police Forces." *Washington Post*. Washington Post, 5 Oct. 2016. Web. 7 Nov. 2016.

6. Ryan Gabrielsen, Ryann Grochowski Jones, and Eric Sagara. "Deadly Force, in Black and White." *ProPublica*. ProPublica, 14 Oct. 2014. Web. 24 Jan. 2017.

7. "Criminal Justice Fact Sheet." *NAACP*. NAACP, n.d. Web. 6 Nov. 2016.

8. Ibid.

9. Ibid.

10. Ibid.

CHAPTER 5. WHITE PRIVILEGE IN EDUCATION

1. Shereen Marisol Meraji. "Before *Brown v. Board*, Mendez Fought California's Segregated Schools." *Morning Edition*. NPR, 16 May 2014. Web. 14 Nov. 2016.

2. Ronald Brownstein. "The Challenge of Educational Inequality." *Atlantic*. Atlantic, 19 May 2016. Web. 24 Jan. 2017.

3. Ibid.

4. "Unequal Education." *Progress 2050*. Center for American Progress, Aug. 2012. Web. 13 Mar. 2017.

5. Ibid.

6. Ronald Brownstein. "The Challenge of Educational Inequality." *Atlantic*. Atlantic, 19 May 2016. Web. 24 Jan. 2017.

7. Jill Rosen. "Teacher Expectations Reflect Racial Biases, Johns Hopkins Study Suggests." *Johns Hopkins Hub*. Johns Hopkins University, 30 Mar. 2016. Web. 27 Jan. 2017.

8. "Civil Rights Data Collection Data Snapshot: School Discipline." *Issue Brief No. 1*. US Department of Education Office for Civil Rights, Mar. 2014. Web. 14 Nov. 2016.

9. Evette A. Simmons-Reed and Gwendolyn Cartledge. "School Discipline Disproportionality: Culturally Competent Interventions for African American Males." *Interdisciplinary Journal of Teaching and Learning* 4.2 (1 June 2004): 98. *Eric*. Web. 8 Nov. 2016.

10. "Civil Rights Data Collection Data Snapshot: School Discipline." *Issue Brief No. 1*. US Department of Education Office for Civil Rights, Mar. 2014. Web. 14 Nov. 2016.

CHAPTER 6. WHITE PRIVILEGE IN THE MEDIA

1. Andrea Mandell. "Oscar Nominations 2017: Diverse Picks Break #OscarsSoWhite." *USA Today*. USA Today, 24 Jan. 2017. Web. 27 Jan. 2017.

2. Maria Puente. "Oscar Nominations 2017: Diversity Is Not a Simple Black-or-White Issue." *USA Today*. USA Today, 25 Jan. 2017. Web. 27 Jan. 2017.

3. David Cox. "#OscarsSoWhite: Who Is Really to Blame for the Oscars' Lack of Diversity?" *Guardian Oscars 2016 Film Blog*. Guardian, 26 Feb. 2017. Web. 27 Jan. 2017.

4. "2015 Hollywood Diversity Report: Flipping the Script." *Ralph J. Bunche Center for African American Studies*. UCLA, 2015. Web. 12 Nov. 2016.

5. Ibid.

6. Keith Chow. "Why Won't Hollywood Cast Asian Actors?" *New York Times*. New York Times, 22 Apr. 2016. Web. 13 Nov. 2016.

7. Yanan Wang. "Rapper Macklemore Checks His White Privilege." *Washington Post*. Washington Post, 25 Jan. 2016. Web. 14 Nov. 2016.

8. Paul Sehgal. "Is Cultural Appropriation Always Wrong?" *New York Times Magazine*. New York Times Magazine, 29 Sept. 2015. Web. 14 Nov. 2016.

SOURCE
NOTES CONTINUED

9. Rudine Sims Bishop. "Mirrors, Windows, and Sliding Glass Doors." *Reading is Fundamental.* Poudre School District, Summer 1990. Web. 14 Nov. 2016.

10. "Publishing Statistics on Children's Books about People of Color and First/Native Nations and by People of Color and First/Native Nations Authors and Illustrators." *CCBC.* University of Wisconsin–Madison, 11 Oct. 2016. Web. 12 Nov. 2016.

CHAPTER 7. WHITE PRIVILEGE AND POLITICS

1. "Civil Rights in America: Racial Voting Rights." *National Park Service.* NPS, 2009. Web. 27 Jan. 2017.

2. "Primary Documents in American History: 15th Amendment to the Constitution." *Library of Congress.* Library of Congress, 17 May 2016. Web. 12 Nov. 2016.

3. Richard H. Pildes and Bradley A. Smith. "The Fifteenth Amendment." *Constitution Center.* Constitution Center, n.d. Web. 12 Nov. 2016.

4. John Lewis. "The Voting Rights Act: Ensuring Dignity and Democracy." *Human Rights Magazine.* American Bar Association, Spring 2005. Web. 12 Nov. 2016.

5. Ari Berman. "The GOPs Attack on Voting Rights Was the Most Under-covered Story of 2016." *Nation.* Nation, 9 Nov. 2016. Web. 14 Nov. 2016.

6. Ibid.

7. Mark Joseph Stern. "Alabama's Failure of Moral Turpitude." *Slate.* Slate, 6 Oct. 2016. Web. 12 Nov. 2016.

8. Ibid.

9. Ibid.

10. Ibid.

11. "Flint Michigan Crisis 'Not Just about Water,' UN Rights Experts Say Ahead of President Obama's Visit." *UN News Centre.* United Nations, 3 May 2016. Web. 12 Nov. 2016.

12. Karl Kurtz. "Who We Elect: The Demographics of State Legislatures." *State Legislatures Magazine.* National Conference of State Legislatures, Dec. 2015. Web. 28 Jan. 2017.

13. Jens Manuel Krogstad. "114th Congress Is Most Diverse Ever." *Fact Tank*. Pew Research Center, 12 Jan. 2015. Web. 14 Nov. 2016.

14. Aaron Blakem. "Yes, Politics Is Still Dominated by Old, White Men. Here's Why." *Washington Post*. Washington Post, 3 Sept. 2014. Web. 28 Jan. 2017.

15. Andrew Cohen. "How White Users Made Heroin a Public-Health Problem." *Atlantic*. Atlantic, 12 Aug. 2015. Web. 28 Jan. 2017.

CHAPTER 8. CRITIQUES OF WHITE PRIVILEGE

1. Dennis Prager. "The Fallacy of White Privilege." *National Review*. National Review, 16 Feb. 2016. Web. 14 Nov. 2016.

2. Gina Crossley-Corcoran. "Explaining White Privilege to a Broke White Person." *Occupy Wall Street*. Occupy Wall Street, n.d. Web. 28 Jan. 2017.

3. David Marcus. "Why White Privilege Is Not the Problem." *Federalist*. Federalist, 9 Jan. 2014. Web. 28 Jan. 2017.

4. Fredrik deBoer. "Admitting That White Privilege Helps You Is Really Just Congratulating Yourself." *Washington Post*. Washington Post, 28 Jan. 2016. Web. 7 Nov. 2016.

5. Mychal Denzel Smith. "White Millennials Are Products of a Failed Lesson in Colorblindness." *PBS News Hour*. PBS, 26 Mar. 2015. Web. 28 Jan. 2017.

CHAPTER 9. MOVING FORWARD

1. Natalia Khosla and Sean McElwee. "White Privilege Has Enormous Implications for Policy—but Whites Don't Think It Exists." *Salon*. Salon, 11 Sept. 2016. Web. 8 Nov. 2016.

2. Ibid.

3. Roxanne Gay. "Only Words." *Toast*. Toast, 25 Nov. 2014. Web. 12 Nov. 2016.

4. "Privilege Walk Lesson Plan." *Peace Learner*. Peace Learner, 14 Mar. 2016. Web. 29 Jan. 2017.

5. Stephen Thrasher. "Claudia Rankine: Why I'm Spending $625,000 to Study Whiteness." *Guardian*. Guardian, 19 Oct. 2016. Web. 24 Oct. 2016.

6. Evette A. Simmons-Reed and Gwendolyn Cartledge. "School Discipline Disproportionality: Culturally Competent Interventions for African American Males." *Interdisciplinary Journal of Teaching and Learning* 4.2 (1 June 2004): 98. *Eric*. Web. 8 Nov. 2016.

7. Chris Mooney. "The Science of Why Cops Shoot Young Black Men." *Mother Jones*. Mother Jones, 1 Dec. 2014. Web. 14 Nov. 2016.

INDEX

ABOUT THE AUTHOR

M. T. Blakemore is an award-winning author and librarian. She lives in Maine with her family.